Workbook and Journal

How To Do The Work

Recognize Your Patterns
Heal from Your Past
and Create Your Self

Book Nerd

ISBN: 9798372996304
ISBN-13:

Table of Contents

Note to readers:
This is an unofficial companion workbook, journal, and summary for Dr. Nicole LePera's How To do The Work. This summary and journal is designed to enrich your reading experience and help you put the principles into action. Buy the original book here: https://www.amazon.com/How-Do-Work-Recognize-Patterns-ebook/dp/B089SZ9JKW/

The information contained in this book has been compiled from sources deemed reliable and it is accurate to the best of the Author's knowledge; however, the Author cannot guarantee its accuracy and validity and cannot be held liable for any errors or omissions. Upon using the information contained in this book, you agree to hold harmless the author from and against any damages, costs, and expenses, including any legal fees, potentially resulting from the application of any of the information provided by this guide. The disclaimer applies to any damages or injury caused by the use and application, whether directly or indirectly, of any advice or information presented, whether for breach of contract, tort, neglect, personal injury, criminal intent, or under any other cause of action. You agree to accept all risks of using the information presented inside this book. The fact that an individual or organization is referred to in this document as a citation or source of information does not imply that the author or publisher endorses the information that the individual or organization provided. This is an unofficial companion journal and summary and has not been approved by the original author of the book.

Introduction

The holistic method involves the physical, psychological, and spiritual aspects of people to help them reconnect with their authentic selves and with the mind, body, and soul. It also involves the epigenome.

Holistic psych helps people find their intuitive voices.

This book has three parts:

1. The foundation
2. The Mind
3. Applied knowledge of self to gain emotional maturity.

Transformation comes from the inside, not from anything out there in the world.

Chapter. 1 Patterns and Root Causes

Have you ever felt stuck in life? Describe a time when you felt stuck like one of Dr. Lepera's clients.

Do you worry about what others think of your patterns and problems?

Do you ever fall back into patterns you aimed to change?

Do you engage in any of these activities? Circle all that apply.

- hyper achievement
- constant travel
- obsession with social media

Was your family emotionally expressive when you were growing up?

How do you show up in life and relationships? Do you notice a common pattern in your life and relationships?

Highlight: Dr. Nicole Lepera believes that the mind-body-soul connection is often omitted in Western medicine.

What do you think of the band-aid model of medicine that treats symptoms instead of the root cause of a problem?

What do you think of genetic determinism and why do people think a disease is part of their identity?

Highlight: Epigenetics is influenced by both the environment and genes. It shows that people aren't helpless and can make a positive impact on their health. Genes don't determine a person's health outcomes.

Have you ever experienced the placebo effect or the nocebo effect? The nocebo effect is the opposite of the placebo effect; it's when a bad event happens as a result of a negative belief about a mediation. Basically, it means patients are more likely to have a severe reaction to a medicine or intervention when they believe it will cause them harm. Do you believe intervention should be forced on people or not?

How do you feel about the story of the young man who overdosed on placebo pills and was taken to the hospital?

Are you willing to become an active participant in your healthcare, do the inner work, and keep consistent habits?

Do you ever betray yourself? How so?

Chapter. 2 Intuition and Patterns

Are you stuck in any destructive behaviors such as drinking or smoking?

Do you have a strong intuition, and do you trust it?

We all have subconscious behavior patterns.

Have you ever felt uncomfortable or agitated when you tried to create change? How so?

What do you think of the study by Ellen Langer? Are you connected to your authentic self, and what impact do your thoughts have on you?

Practice being in the present moment for at least a few minutes a day.

Chapter. 3 The Theory of Trauma

The ACE test is used to measure trauma. Here is one version of the test that you may take:
https://americanspcc.org/take-the-aces-quiz/
We are not affiliated with the above link so feel free to take any other valid ACE tests.

The higher a score is, the greater the chance of a negative life outcome, but with intervention, one has a chance of recovering from trauma.

Have you ever experienced a spiritual transformation like Christine has had?

____

____

____

____

____

____

____

____

Describe a time when you felt unworthy or unacceptable when you were a kid. Victims of trauma betray their true selves to survive, and trauma isn't always obvious.

Has a parent figure projected their unresolved trauma onto you? Did you feel seen?

Archetypes of Trauma

Has a parent ever denied your reality? How did you feel?

Did you feel seen and heard when growing up?

Do you have any trouble with making decisions? Were you ever obsessed with success? If yes, you may have had a parent who tried to live vicariously through you.

Have you known any parents who talk behind the

backs of their partners to their children? Or a parent who doesn't respect personal space?

Have you seen parents who were overly focused on appearance or criticized people's looks right in front of you?

Do you know of any parents who were distant or emotionally withdrawn from their kids?

What is the biggest trauma of your childhood? You may recall a moment or year of your life that changed you.

There are two ways of coping:

Adaptive coping- A way of coping that makes one feel safe again after a challenge. It includes dealing with problems directly.

Maladaptive coping- Includes unhealthy distractions of dissociation to deal with problems. The most common maladaptive ways to cope with problems include dissociation, rage, anger, and people-pleasing. This method includes preserving oneself or one's life circumstances.

Chapter. 4 Trauma in the Body

Do you experience chronic stress? If yes, what effects does it have on your body?

____

____

____

____

____

____

____

____

Highlight: The autonomic nervous system takes care of basic involuntary functions of the body while the parasympathetic nervous system regulates higher executive functions.

When was the last time you had a fight, flight, or freeze reaction to something?

____

____

____

____

____

Highlight: A poor vagal tone can lead to higher sensitivity to an environment's threats, be they real or imagined. This can lead to relationship troubles and a feeling of disconnection.

Did you grow up in a calm or chaotic environment?

Chapter. 5 Healing the Mind and Body

Highlight: SSRIs are created in the brain as well as in the gut.

Have you ever suffered from gut dysbiosis or a leaky gut from eating too many greasy foods? Gut dysbiosis can lead to physical and mental illness.

Highlight: Intermittent fasting and nutrient-dense foods are beneficial for the body and vagal tone.
A research study called The New Science of the Lost Art showed that lung span is the biggest indicator of life span.

Do you enjoy singing, dancing, or playing video games? These activities help the nervous system.

Which midfrequency music have you listened to that opens up your middle ear and puts you in a happy place?

Chapter. 6 Belief is Powerful

Beliefs are established through real-life experiences that are practiced. What are some beliefs of yours that you feel are getting in the way of you living a full life?

Highlight: The deepest insights about your identity make up your core beliefs.

Which negative criticism from your life is most memorable to you or sticks in your mind?

Children go through an egocentric stage where they're not able to distinguish between the self and others. Do you still blame yourself for something that happened in childhood?

Do you have a hard time caring for yourself without feeling selfish or always comparing yourself to others? This may be due to a core belief you developed in childhood. Which belief about yourself would you like to replace with a more empowering one?

Chapter. 7 Meeting Your Inner Child

The 4 attachment styles:

Secure- The results of a positive and stable home. A child is socially engaged and doesn't feel anxious for a long period nor avoids the mother.

Avoidant- Child doesn't show signs of stress. Avoids the mom. Children with this attachment style are emotionally neglected and don't rely on their parents for emotional support.

Anxious/ resistant- An aching attachment style that's hard to soothe. People with this style crave lots of attention.

Disorganized/disoriented- No predictable attachment style. A child in this environment has been traumatized and doesn't know how to find safety. This is a sign they live in a chaotic or disorganized environment.

When do you feel unseen, unheard, or unloved?

Highlight: Childhood trauma creates subconscious inner child wounds that are the result of unmet spiritual, physical, or emotional needs.

7 inner child archetypes:

1. The caretaker- gains self-worth and a sense of self by ignoring one's own needs.
2. The overachiever- seeks external validation to bolster low self-worth.
2. The underachiever- keeps oneself invisible and small to gain love.
3. The rescuer/ protector- gains love by protecting others and catering to their needs.
4. The life of the party- feels like they need to keep everyone happy to feel loved.
5. The 'yes' person- takes care of others' needs while neglecting their own and is willing to "drop everything" for others.
6. The hero worshiper- follows a guide or guru and believes it's best to model others' ways of life rather than listen to the self.

Do you have any escapist fantasies of wanting to escape your life?

Do you feel good enough without seeking validation from people? That's an important goal to have according to the author.

Chapter. 8 The Ego and Its Stories

Highlight: The ego is the protector of the inner child and identifies as "I." It protects our identity no matter what.

What is your ego telling you about your identity?

What opinions of yours have been questioned? Did you feel threatened?

What barriers has the ego placed in your life?

The ego can show up in these ways:

- through a strong emotional reaction
- narcissistic behavior
- seeing the world in extremes, i.e. right vs. wrong with no room for gray areas
- extreme competition

Do you feel threatened as a person when your beliefs are threatened?

When people feel invalidated, they feel their worth is destroyed. A relationship will feel less conflicting when two people find a shared truth instead of fighting to establish their own power and worth.

What do you see as bad or wrong about yourself? These are the parts of you in the shadows.

Does any part of you feel repressed or inauthentic?

What did you learn about your ego after you did Nicole's exercise?

____

____

____

____

____

____

____

____

Chapter. 9 Trauma Bonds

Signs of a trauma bond:

- obsession with problematic relationships due to the excitement they exude which feels like love
- unawareness of one's own needs or rarely addressing one's needs in a relationship
- self-betrayal and lack of self-trust

Archetypes of trauma bonds:

- parents who deny a child's reality and thus create a void in their life
- parents who don't see nor hear a child
- parents who live vicariously through their kids or shape them in ways that they find pleasing
- parents who don't model boundaries
- parents who focus too much on looks
- parents who can't control their own emotions

Do any of these child-parent dynamics sound familiar to you? A person's parent-child bond may be recreated in a future relationship.

Highlight: A mutually fulfilling and authentic relationship allows both parties to evolve and feel seen, heard, and expressive. It's peaceful but not necessarily romantic.

Chapter. 10 Boundaries

Did you ever experience enmeshment or no separation between your family's and your own opinions?

Are you withdrawn from others and put up a wall or do you have no boundaries?

Highlight: If you have a hard time asking for help, are

afraid of rejection, and have few friends then your walls are likely too rigid. If you have a hard time saying "no," if you overshare, and if you are a chronic people-pleaser then your boundaries are too low.

Types of boundaries: physical, resource boundaries, mental, and emotional boundaries

Did your family have loose or rigid boundaries when you were growing up?

Do you overshare or have you been in a conversation with someone who overshares?

Has anyone dumped their feelings on you without getting a sense of your mood? Have you commiserated with someone by dumping a shared problem on them?

Are you good at maintaining your boundaries? Who pushes your boundaries?

Have you ever had to cut ties with someone because they were toxic?

Do you have a hard time maintaining your boundaries without feeling selfish or mean? Or are you good at keeping boundaries?

Chapter. 11 Reparenting

Highlight: Being spiritually awakened activates the same neural pathways that depression activates in the brain.

Have you ever experienced a spiritual transformation like Dr. Lepera has?

Children want to express themselves and feel safe to have their spiritual, physical, and emotional needs met. Which of your needs do you feel your parents met?

How people with childhood wounds protect their egos:

- They try to be right while rejecting the opinions of others
- By wearing a mask
- By avoiding intimacy
- By clinging to intimacy

What are some of your unmet needs?

4 pillars of reparenting:

1. emotional regulation
2. loving discipline
3. self-care
4. rediscovering your childhood sense of wonder

How will you incorporate these four pillars into your life?

Will you have an honest discussion with your parents about your reparenting journey and past wrongs?

Name a few times in your life when you listened to your inner self and addressed your needs.

What do you need most at this point?

What are your rituals and daily routines?

What's something imaginative or new that you want to try?

Chapter. 12 Emotions and Maturity

Do you focus too much on how others perceive you? If you're too focused on perception, it might mean that you were raised in a home that didn't allow you to express yourself fully.

Do you know of people who are uncomfortable with emotional expression and lash out or shut down when others show emotions?

Do you believe that your opinions and reality are valid by themselves? Are you ok with being misunderstood? Accepting that not everyone will understand you signals maturity.

What do you think of emotional tolerance and tolerating all of your feelings?

Highlight: Emotions last physiologically for 90 seconds at which point the body tries to return to homeostasis, as long as the mind doesn't get in the way.

Have you ever kept a grudge for months and couldn't stop ruminating or do emotions flow through you without being held back?

Some self-soothing activities that worked for the author include moving her body, taking a walk, taking a bath, or reading. These activities might help you discharge or you may have to try them out if you aren't sure. How good are you at tolerating stress- do you remain calm or freak out?

How can a parent stay balanced, stay authentic, and regulate one's emotions?

Do you feel secure and safe to make mistakes?

Here are some self-soothing activities: bathing, getting a massage, reading, writing, engaging with music, and cuddling.

Activities for emotional endurance: resting, using the five senses, breathing, enjoying nature, praying, repeating affirmations, engaging in a temporary distraction, speaking with a supportive person

Chapter 13. Interdependence

What do you think of the author's self-pity story and how she didn't want to go to the beach? Was it wise of her to go and join her partner?

Do you trust your inner world? Do you have supportive relationships?

Is your nervous system regulated and do you feel safe enough to connect with others?

How do you think humanity should start letting go of 'us v. them' thinking?

Coloring Pages

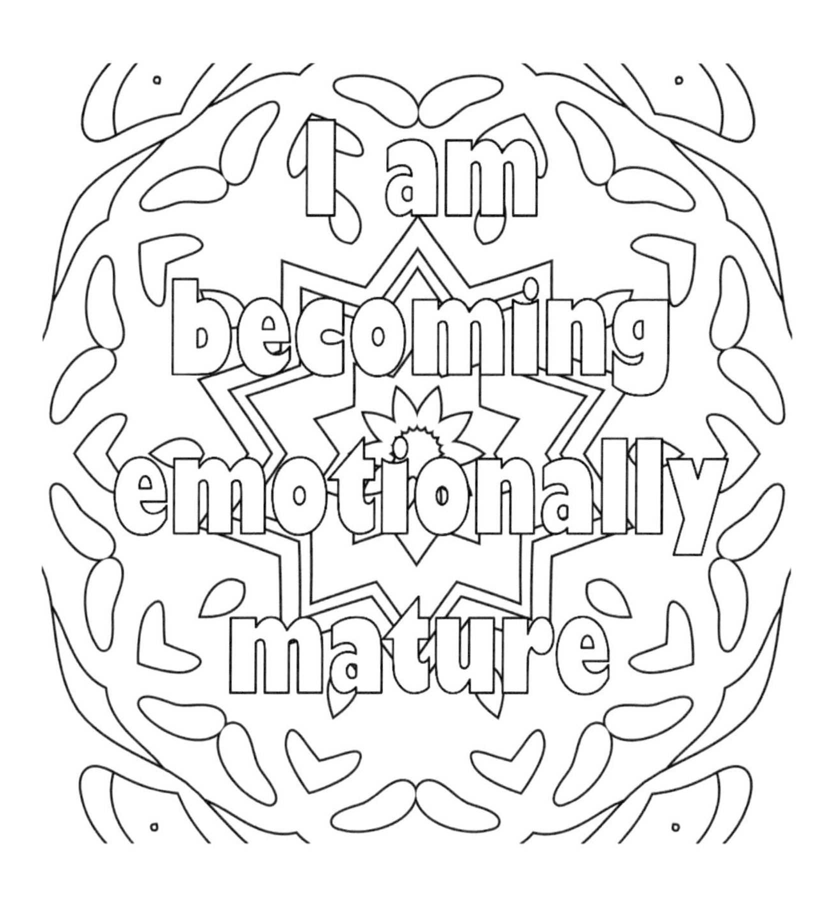

My reactions
are grounded
and I make
concious
choices

I am
grateful for
the peace
in my life

My
attention
is on the
present
moment

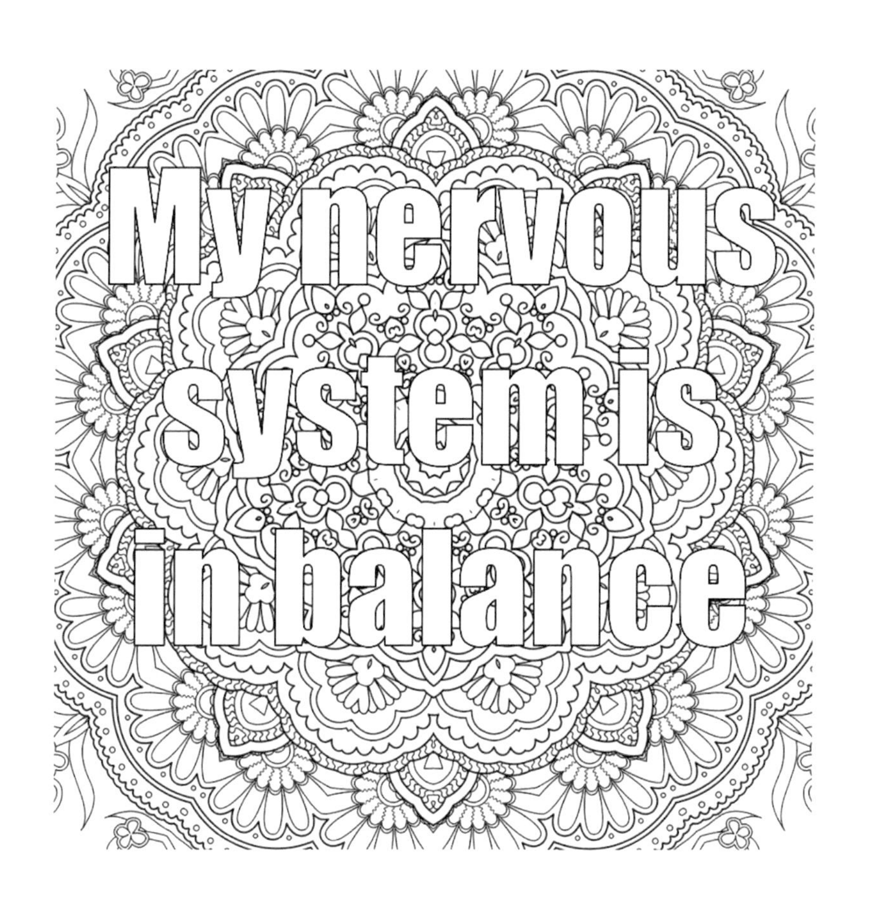
My nervous
system is
in balance

Congrats on getting through the journal! If you found it insightful and discovered something new about yourself, please post a review and describe your experience. Your review will help us create more journals for you to enjoy in the future.

Book Nerd team

Made in the USA
Thornton, CO
01/20/24 10:30:10

32254a62-f112-4eed-ba49-c48497939713R01